The
Garland Library
of
War and Peace

The Garland Library of War and Peace

War

by

Kerr Eby

with a new introduction
for the Garland Edition by
Charles Chatfield

Garland Publishing, Inc., New York & London
1971

Library of Congress Cataloging in Publication Data

Eby, Kerr, 1890-1946.
War.

(The Garland library of war and peace)
Reprint of the 1936 ed.
1. European war, 1914-1918--Pictorial works.
I. Title. II. Series.
NE2012.E28A57 1971 760'.0924 75-147683
ISBN 0-8240-0440-X

Printed in the United States of America

Introduction

Kerr Eby himself introduced this book. But what of Eby? He has acknowledged that his etchings were drawn from experience, from sketches or from indelible memories of World War I. He was there, having enlisted in 1917 and having been a sergeant in the Army Corps of Engineers until 1919. He was prepared when he entered the service to render it through art for posterity.

Eby was born in Tokyo in 1890, and he lived there three years. His father was a Methodist missionary from Canada, and the family moved frequently upon returning from Japan. His mother was a daughter of Frederick Keppel, senior member of the art firm of Frederick Keppel and Son, and Eby committed himself to the study of art from an early age. As a youth he worked as a "printer's devil" for a country newspaper, a job which may have influenced the form of art that he would adopt as his own, etching.

He came to the United States in 1907. In New York City he studied art at the Pratt Institute and he worked nights at the Art Students League, taking a job at the American Lithographic Company. By the time of World War I Eby had held several jobs and experimented with a variety of drawing techniques; that is to say, he had tested experience and ways of recording it.

Eby had an uncle, Frederick P. Keppel, who as Assistant Secretary of War presumably had an overview of the war effort, but the young man saw it on its lowest terms. He got the whole and genuine meanness of it, and published its meanness to the world. He brought back drawings and sketches made at the front and for a decade he drew upon them. Increasingly, he rendered the war in two senses: he transmitted the war experience visually, but also he extracted from it, melted it down into human terms, and clarified its meaning. In the thirties the ominous clouds of a new general war crystallized Eby's outrage with the first one and led to the compilation of this volume.

Originally printed and circulated privately, War *was published by Yale University Press in 1936. Dorothy Noyes Arms, the wife of artist John Taylor Arms with whom Eby occasionally worked, wrote appreciatively that his war subjects "have the widest range of technical expression" of all his works.*[1] *The collection includes lithographs, dry-points, drawings, and pure etchings. Eby made the most of the essential qualities of each medium: the weariness of landscape and blurring of individuality is conveyed through lithograph; stark, dramatic contrasts of action and values are established through dry-point; the ironies of combat and the somber lines of wasted death are*

[1] *Dorothy Noyes Arms, "Kerr Eby, A.N.A.,"* American Etchers, *VIII (New York: The Grafton Collection, Inc., 1930), n.p.*

suggested by drawing; clarity of observation is fixed through etching. Wrote Mrs. Arms:

> *They were etched when the horror and nobleness, ruin and tragic beauty of it all were fresh and vivid things in Mr. Eby's memory. Then came the reaction against all reminders of those days, and peaceful scenes and tranquil subjects held sway, until now, in 1929, there appears a new war plate, "The Caissons Go Rolling Along." It is retrospective and quite different, for whereas the earlier plates were the delineation of some definite scene or event, this one seems a symbol. It is the epitome of war; a composite memory which has lain fallow, then matured during the passage of the peace-filled years . . . The technical mastery is complete, so much so that one can and does forget it and is carried away by the sheer dramatic beauty of the whole. It is war itself, seen through the eyes of an artist, and reproduced for all time by his most skilful hand.*[2]

Every owner of this book will form attachments to specific plates. The last, September 13, 1918, *is a vivid, sweeping view of the St. Mihiel drive from the Allied side, the scene dominated by a great cloud that hung for days above the troops. According to Dorothy Keppel, writing of Eby, a German seeing drawings of this subject recalled the cloud and said that on his side it was deep red and was called by German troops "The Cloud of Blood."*[3] *Like many*

[2] Ibid.

[3] *Dorothy Keppel, "Kerr Eby,"* The Print Collector's Quarterly, *XXVI (1939), p. 91.*

of the plates in this book, it communicates the battle-loneliness experienced by masses of men together.

Between the wars Eby chose a wide variety of predominantly natural subjects for his art. He produced one series of plates on a return trip to Europe, but he drew most of his inspiration from New England, especially Connecticut where he made his home. Most often his subject was nature itself, and he delighted particularly in handling snow scenes, perhaps because they are so largely lines to begin with. Snow has simplified the matter, and the natural design presents itself directly to the artist's eyes.

Design is an aesthetic Grail, of course, but for Eby it was more than that; it appears to have been the counterpart of his own individualism. Mrs. Arms wrote, with reason to know, that design was "the principle to which, in all its purity and loveliness, he had dedicated his art. One senses this in every plate; the searching for the perfect pattern."[4]

War is the antithesis of this principle; it is chaos and destruction. But it is not therefore meaningless; and when the war he rued swept over the world again, Kerr Eby enlisted his talents, seeking meaning in the lives and deaths of the men who fought it in the Pacific. As an artist-correspondent he accompanied the United States Marines, covering the landing on the beaches of Tarawa and the fighting in the jungles of Bougainville and elsewhere. In 1945 he exhibited

[4] *Arms, "Kerr Eby."*

at the Galleries of the Associated American Artists a collection which was hailed as one of the finest to have come out of the war. He died in Westport, Connecticut, the following year, on November 19, 1946.[5]

Kerr Eby was dedicated to art, and was a member of the National Academy of Design, the Institute of Arts and Letters, and other professional associations. He had a deep attachment to his nation, its natural setting and its people, which was revealed in his work. He was keenly interested in politics, we are told, but was not rigid in his affiliations. He abhorred war, but he never became detached from it. Unlike most war advocates and, unfortunately, unlike many war protesters, he never abstracted war. This collection of his works is important precisely because it renders warfare in its human – and inhuman – dimensions.

Charles Chatfield
Department of History
Wittenberg University

[5] *Kerr Eby was survived by his wife, Phyllis Barretto, of California and New York, whom he had married in 1935. His first wife, Frances Sheldon, had died in 1932 after twelve years of marriage.*

WAR

BY

KERR EBY

NEW HAVEN
YALE UNIVERSITY PRESS
1936

Printed in the United States of America

DEDICATED

To those who gave their lives for an idea,
the men who never came back.

CONTENTS

INTRODUCTION

Ernest started trumpeting, and cracked his manger,
Leonard started roaring, and shivered his stall,
James gave the huffle of a snail in danger,
And nobody heard him at all.

A. A. Milne

I WRITE in all humility of spirit, in the desperate hope that somehow it may be of use in the forlorn and seemingly hopeless fight against war. About the prints and drawings in this book I make no comment, save that they were made from the indelible impressions of war. They are not imaginary. I saw them.

I have been accused of being a pacifist. Just what constitutes a pacifist is rather vague in my mind. I am not a pacifist if it means not to see the necessity of an army and navy in this world as it is and not to thank God for them. If it is to keep turning the other cheek like the pivoted head of an owl, I have not reached that state of Christian forbearance but I most certainly am a pacifist if being one is to believe that there can be and are other ways of settling differences between Christian nations than murdering youngsters—and that lawful, not to say sanctified, wholesale slaughter is simply slobbering imbecility.

I saw a great deal of America's part in the last war by an accident of service. In our army anything that was queer or out of the way was put onto the Engineers, so we of the Camouflage working with and attached to the field artillery were engineers, the 40th Regiment of the regular army. There were comparatively few of us divided into groups of ten or twelve men to a regiment of artillery. We had few replacements and of necessity when our division of the moment was withdrawn from the line for rest and replacements we of the Camouflage were transferred to the incoming outfit and stayed with them in action. How many divisions had the doubtful blessing of my services I cannot remember nor the names of the places we went—all that is a haze—but what I do remember and brilliantly—is what it looked like and felt like. The men like maggots in a cheese—and seemingly moving as aimlessly. The feeling of the night movements. The endless walking in a semi-coma with perhaps your hand on a gun barrel to keep you steady with always the danger of going to sleep on your feet and being crushed by a caisson behind—all these things, the endless piling up of the minutia of the human side of war I remember. And on the advances, the dead. Singly or in windrows—always the dead youngsters—the period to what we were doing. It seemed idiotic to me even then. It seems doubly idiotic to me now.

There was great beauty in the last war as there is always beauty in human giving, but the beauty was in the giver not in the thing itself. It must be remembered that all of us underneath had some vague idea of purging the world of an evil. It was always there submerged under our profane bellyaching and fooling about anything and everything. It seemed almost right that those still, shapeless bundles should be there—that something new and good should come of it. Now we know that nothing came of it—much to the contrary—they died for less than nothing. We who are left have seen to that.

The world today is a more savage place than the world of 1914. Those of us who remember anything before that year know this. By no stretch of the imagination was it a perfect place then but by comparison it was far more gentle. There is immeasurably more hate and distrust everywhere now and far less hope. We as youngsters before 1914 had at least a fighting chance to do what we wanted to do. Given enough stuff on the ball and hard work we felt that we could go somewhere. We did not have that blighting sense of being just one too many that so many of the young ones of today must feel. I should hate to be starting now. All this an inheritance of war and what men died for. Hell! I'd like to hear what they would say.

Now less than twenty years after, having learned nothing, done nothing, we actually have it plastered before our noses—"The handwriting on the wall"—that, barring a God-sent miracle, there is to be another war. Stop and think—this is not just crying "Wolf." The thing is right there—we all know it—and know that it can break like lightning as in 'fourteen. We know it and as people we do nothing.

The last war was to me, as to most of my generation, a profoundly moving adventure. Certainly since the armistice it has been a continuous source of grist for my particular mill. At first I thought of it as just that but of late years I have had a growing feeling that we who know something of what war means should get up on our hind legs and do or say what we can.

Years ago Bateman in *London Punch* had a piercingly funny set of drawings entitled "The One-Note Man." It starts the day of a member of a symphony orchestra very early in the morning. He gets up, takes exercises, gargles his throat, blows things up his nose and makes innumerable preparations. It carries him all through the day, into the hall, nearly through the symphony—till the moment of all moments arrives—up goes his horn and out comes his one note. The one note needed to make perfect the great work. After that with an expression of ineffable peace at duty well done he goes home to bed. You all know the terrific power of mass formation in anything, of mass thinking. It's a copybook truism. Damn it, surely this thing is important enough to most of us. It has nothing to do with creed or race or color. Surely it touches us all vitally enough to tootle our one note. Tootle them all together and by God there would be such a blast of good fresh air as would blow the foul smell of war out of existence.

I haven't much to say against fighting for those who like it. I am no evangelist. What I am stewed up about is the incredible folly of supposedly Christian nations putting all their efficiency, ingenuity and strength into the business of tearing out each other's throats, and at the same time every one of them calling for help and power to do it on the same God—through His only Son, the Prince of Peace. It's a staggering spectacle. It actually seems that as our science progresses our humanities and common sense crumble. We were very, very good at the business of killing in the last war. We will be unthinkable in the next.

The extraordinary thing is that in the whole world there is probably not one sane person who, left alone, wants war. The very great majority of us stand to lose all that we hold most dear. Yet all we seem capable of is to sit on our behinds, doing nothing—and watch with sheeplike eyes the slaughter creeping nearer.

I have no more definite idea of what can be done than anyone else, but there is one great latent power, unused, capable of anything. A power old as life. I speak of the protective instinct of any she-thing for her young. A gentle tabby cat to protect her kittens will land all fury and claws on the nose of a mastiff. I have seen it. Hurt any baby thing and watch out for the mother. The most chilled steel act of courage of my experience was that of a mother mouse. Years ago in my attic at the top of an old trunk filled with clothes, I found a nest of field mice with five naked squirming infants. As I lifted the lid away went the parents, the father for parts unknown. I was interested in the little brutes and was peering at them only inches away. There was a rustle along the edge of the trunk, right under my godlike nose came the mother. Looking me straight in the eye she took a baby and carried it away to safety. Five times she did it, expecting every moment to be her last. That's guts.

You women. I am speaking wholly to you now. The gentlest of you have that quality in a pinch. Is it not possible to use it for your own? Is it not possible somehow to get together in your millions and raise hell about this thing all over the world? You could be irresistible. We males, most of us, in this kind of thing are handicapped. It is the tradition of the race that we should be bold. We are afraid to be afraid or seem to be afraid. We have got to try to be nonchalant even though we are about to shake out of our pants. You women have no such inhibitions. You don't have to be men. You don't have to be brave gentlemen, and if you are moved enough you don't even have to be ladies. Can't you be afraid enough for your own sons to do something? Afraid enough to try to keep them from being turned into bloated hunks of human meat in the springtime of their lives?

Most of my friends have sons, big and strong, with torsos like wedges and stomachs like washboards. One strokes a crew, another is a shark at sailing small boats and so on. You mothers who breed that kind remember this—they are the first to go always. You have given them all you have. You have watched them from the time they were little helpless red things chewing their toes. Watched them as their legs stretched out long and straight and their chests turned into barrels. Watched them until you must look up at them not down, and been so proud. Can't you do something that will allow them to be more than a memory and a little white cross in those ghastly acres of the dead? Let them live for their country, not die for it.

I was a very big youngster towering over my own mother. I can so well remember when in a sort of inward ecstasy she took me by the lapels and shaking me gently said almost to herself, "You big lump. You must be a fine man. You have just got to be a fine man or I won't be able to bear it." You all feel that way. Can't you do something not only to let them be fine as you want them to be, but just to be men?

You younger women and girls. For so many of you if war comes life will be made very simple indeed. So simple that it will hardly be worth living. There will be no one for so many of you to love. I read somewhere that in the last war there were altogether seventeen million men lost. That means probably the frustrated lives of a like number of your sisters of my generation. Every one of you has her hopes and her dreams. Surely your dream and your life are worth fighting for.

I do not know what definite means can be used to prevent another war but I do know that anything that can be done must be done before it breaks. It is like a disease when it comes, attacking us all. You will give up your lives or your sons or your lovers. You will do what you are told and like it. I will probably wave a flag, a fire-eating fool.

It is said that war is human nature—that we always have had wars and always will—I do not believe it. Something can be done about it. God knows it is human nature to have syphilis. Nothing could be done about it but to die horribly until one man after six hundred and six tries found that something could be done. Maybe there is no one thing that can prevent another war but I do know that if everyone who has any feeling in the matter at all said what he felt in no uncertain terms—and kept saying it—the sheer power of public opinion would go far to make war impossible. I am a very profane man. I am not being profane now when I say, "For Christ's sake, say or do what you can!"

KERR EBY

A KISS FOR THE KAISER

AN ARTILLERY TRAIN

IN THE OPEN

REFUGEES

DAWN; THE 75'S FOLLOW UP

INFANTRY; CHÂTEAU-THIERRY

A BIT OF THE ARGONNE

SCOUT PLANES AT DAWN

STUCK

ROUGH GOING

SHADOWS

BARRAGE

THE NIGHT MARCH

OPEN ACTION

WHERE DO WE GO?

THE CAISSONS GO ROLLING ALONG

PENCIL SELLERS, CLASS OF '17

THEY HUNT NO MORE!

VICTORY

THE LAST SUPPER

CAMOUFLAGE

MARKED FOR BURIAL

THE GOLDEN RULE

UNKNOWN SOLDIER

ONE OF OURS

A BIT OF THE ARGONNE, NO. 2

MAMA'S BOY

SEPTEMBER 13, 1918. SAINT-MIHIEL